Children's Sermons for Church Celebrations

CHILDREN'S SERMONS
FOR CHURCH CELEBRATIONS

Roy E. De Brand

NASHVILLE, TENNESSEE

© Copyright 1990 • Broadman Press
All Rights Reserved
4260-32
ISBN: 0-8054-6032-2
Dewey Decimal Classification: 252.53
Subject Headings: CHILDREN'S SERMONS
Library of Congress Catalog Number: 90-33980
Printed in the United States of America

Unless otherwise noted, all Scripture quotations are taken from the *Revised Standard Version of the Bible*, copyrighted 1946, 1952, © 1971, 1973.

All Scripture notations marked (GNB) are from the *Good News Bible*, the Bible in Today's English Version. Old Testament: Copyright © American Bible Society 1976; New Testament: Copyright © American Bible Society 1966, 1971, 1976. Used by permission.

All Scripture notations marked (KJV) are from the *King James Version* of the Bible.

Library of Congress Cataloging-in-Publication Data

De Brand, Roy E.
    Children's sermons for church celebrations / Roy E. De Brand.
       p.   cm.
    ISBN 0-8054-6032-2
    1. Children's sermons. 2.Occasional sermons. 3. Church year sermons.   I. Title.
BV4315.D36   1991
252'.53--dc20

90-33980
CIP

TO CAROLYN
with whom to celebrate life
daily is ultimate joy

Contents

Suggested Chronological Calendar for the Year 11
Preface 15
1. Advent (Preparation for Christmas)
   A Time of Hope............................. 18
   A Time of Giving............................ 19
   A Time of Seeking........................... 20
   A Time of Getting........................... 21
2. Bible Study Week
   How the Bible Helps Us 22
3. Christmas
   Understanding Jesus for Yourself................ 24
4. Christian Home Week
   What Makes a House a Home? 26
5. Church Music Week
   We Have a Song to Sing!...................... 27
6. Deacon Election
   Servants of the Lord 29
7. Easter
   A Symbol of Life 31
8. Epiphany Sunday
   Finding What You're Looking For 32
9. Father's Day
   How to Honor Your Father 33
10. Foreign Missions Sunday
    Little Things Are Important, Too!............... 35
11. Good Friday
    Who Is Good Friday Good For? 37
12. Graduation Sunday
    An Important Step in Life 38

13. Home Missions Sunday
    Putting on Our "Jesus Glasses" 40
14. Labor Day
    Be the Best Worker You Can Be 42
15. Lent (Preparation for Easter)
    The Hand of Love 44
    The Voice of Love 45
    The Gift of Love 45
    The Prayer of Love 46
    The Mind of Love 47
    The Joy of Love 48
16. Lord's Supper
    A Timeless Reminder 49
    Has Everyone Been Served? 50
    A Strange Time for Singing 51
    Do You See a Reflection? 52
17. Maundy Thursday
    How Love Is Measured 54
18. Memorial Day
    A Different Beatitude 56
19. Mother's Day
    Mothers Know Best 58
20. New Year's Sunday
    What to Lose and What to Seek 59
21. Old Year's Sunday
    Old and New—Side by Side 61
22. Palm Sunday
    A Parade for Jesus 63
23. Pentecost Sunday
    The Birthday of the Church 65

24. Race Relations Sunday
    Outside, Inside, and All Over................... 67
25. Religious Liberty Sunday
    Let Freedom Ring!............................ 69
26. Revival
    How Do We Change?......................... 71
27. Senior Adult Day
    They've Been Where We Haven't............... 73
28. Stewardship Promotion
    Put on a Happy Face.......................... 75
29. Sunday School Promotion Day
    The Girl Who Wouldn't Promote 77
30. Thanksgiving
    Everybody but Turkeys Give Thanks............. 79
31. Trinity Sunday
    How Do You Picture God? 80
32. Valentine's Day
    Horace the Horrible........................... 82
33. Women's Day
    The Strength of Steel.......................... 84
34. World Hunger Sunday
    The House on the Hill......................... 86
35. World Peace Sunday
    The Peace Pipe............................... 88
36. World Prayer Sunday
    At the Sound of Your Name 90
37. Youth Week
    Pretending or Preparing?....................... 91
Index of Scripture Texts 93

Suggested Chronological Calendar for the Year

Advent—begins the fourth Sunday before Christmas Day and proceeds consecutively throughout the following Sundays until Christmas.

Foreign Missions Sunday—is the second Sunday in December in many denominations.

Christmas—is December 25 or is celebrated the Sunday closest to it.

Old Year's Sunday—is the last Sunday of the old year (the Sunday between Christmas and the New Year).

Epiphany Sunday—is January 6 or the closest Sunday.

New Year's Sunday—is January 1 or is celebrated the first Sunday of the new year.

Bible Study Week—is often the first full week in January or another week in close proximity.

Valentine's Day—is the Sunday preceding or closest to February 14.

Women's Day—is the second Sunday in February for some groups.

Race Relations Sunday—is the second or third Sunday in February, depending on denomination.

Lent—begins on Ash Wednesday (forty weekdays before Easter) and concludes at noon on the Saturday of Holy Week.

World Prayer Sunday—is the first Sunday of Lent.

Home Missions Sunday—is the second Sunday in March for many groups.

Youth Week—is designated by some denominations as the second week of March.

Palm Sunday—is one week before Easter and begins Holy Week.

Maundy Thursday—is the Thursday before Easter.

Good Friday—is the Friday before Easter.

Easter—begins at sunrise on the designated Sunday in March or April.

Senior Adult Day—is the first Sunday in May for some denominations.

Mother's Day—is the second Sunday in May.

Christian Home Week—is traditionally the week beginning with Mother's Day.

Memorial Day— is celebrated the Sunday before May 30 or the date Memorial Day is observed.

Graduation Sunday—is the first Sunday in June or another late May or early June Sunday.

Father's Day—is the third Sunday in June.

Pentecost Sunday—is the seventh Sunday after Easter.

Trinity Sunday—is the eighth Sunday after Easter.

Religious Liberty Sunday—is July 4 or the Sunday preceding it.

Suggested Chronological Calendar for the Year 13

World Peace Sunday—is the first Sunday in August.

Church Music Week—is the third week in August for some groups.

Labor Day—is the Sunday before the first Monday in September.

Deacon Election—is generally in the early fall, but may be at any time.

Revival—is traditionally in the fall or spring.

Stewardship Promotion—is traditionally in the fall, but may be at any time.

Sunday School Promotion Sunday—is the first Sunday in October traditionally, but in many churches coincides with the opening of school.

World Hunger Sunday—is the second Sunday in October.

Thanksgiving—is the Sunday preceding Thanksgiving Day.

Lord's Supper—is whenever your church celebrates it—monthly, quarterly, and so forth.

Preface

Churches celebrate a lot. This is the way it should be, because celebration is foundational to all we do and all we are as the church of Jesus Christ. We celebrate who Jesus was and what He did. We celebrate special occasions like Jesus' birth (Christmas), death (Good Friday), and resurrection (Easter). Even the day on which we worship was changed to celebrate Jesus' resurrection. We celebrate the great, central truths of our faith in song and sermon. We celebrate God's grace, fully given through Jesus Christ. We celebrate the Lord's Supper and baptism, the two things Jesus asked us to celebrate perpetually to remember Him. We celebrate each other. When something good and significant happens in the lives of church members—like graduation, ordination, or marriage—we celebrate these special events, too. We often eat together as the family of God, celebrating by being together and enjoying one another's company. Celebration plays a big part in the life of the church.

Children also like to celebrate. Go to any six-year-old's birthday party and be reminded of this fact, if you've forgotten. Watch children at Christmas, Easter, or even in Sunday School and worship. Sometimes moms or dads have to put the "quietus" on children's celebrations in church so that others won't be disturbed. Celebration is a significant factor of childhood.

We should celebrate children. They are truly God's gifts to us. Our celebration of God's gifts should be a regular practice in church. Children's sermons come from this idea. To include children in worship by having a gospel lesson on their level of understanding is to honor them indeed. There is, in my opinion, no greater way to honor, celebrate, or love children in the church than this. No one can do any better thing for children than to present the gospel of Jesus Christ to them. Come, celebrate children with me. Come, celebrate the good news on a child's level. To these ends, this book is lovingly directed.

As you use this book remember that the ideas in it are meant to be suggestive. Obviously, you'll have to adapt them to your own situation and needs. Some of them may have to be altered significantly. That's OK. Please don't *just* retell my experiences, as if they were yours. Use the ideas to relate things from your own experiences or give credit where credit is due. This is easy to do; "I read about a preacher who . . ." is a way. If I have given you even the seed of an idea, I will be happy. I'm always scouting for good ideas for children's sermons. I hope I've supplied you with some in this volume.

One of my intentions with this volume is to provide you with enough ideas for virtually a whole year of children's sermons. I've gone through denominational calendars, the liturgical calendar, and the annual calendar hoping to cover most of the days emphasized. I know I didn't mention every single emphasis on everybody's list. However, I do think I focused on most of them. Maybe I included some that were not on your list. Whether I did or didn't, I hope you will find help in this volume.

My methods in this volume vary widely. Many of the children's sermons are object centered. Some are story centered. Some are inductive in form; some are narrative; and some are deductive. There are a lot of ways to prepare children's sermons. I hope you'll find some inspiration from what I've done and create your own sermons in various creative forms.

God bless our children!

Thanks to my God-given wife, Carolyn, and to my nearly grown-and-gone children, Brian and DeAnn, for their ideas, love, support, and helpful suggestions in this project.

1
Advent (Preparation for Christmas)

A Time of Hope

Text: Jeremiah 33:14, "Behold, the days are coming, says the Lord, when I will fulfil the promise I made to the house of Israel and the house of Judah."

Main Truth: Before we can celebrate Christmas, we need to get ready.

Interest Object: A cassette tape.

Today is the beginning of a time called Advent, a fancy word that simply means *coming*. It's four Sundays to get ready to celebrate Jesus' coming to earth. This is something we all need to do—get ready for Christmas. It couldn't be nearly as meaningful, not half as much fun, if we just woke up on December 25 and tried to have Christmas without any preparation—no lights, no tree, no Christmas dinner, no gifts. Before we can celebrate Christmas, we need to get ready.

The people in the Bible had to get ready, too. It took a long time for them to get ready for Jesus' birth. In fact, it took hundreds of years, and God did more preparation than the people did. First, God created people in His own image. Then, when people sinned, God planned a way for them to be forgiven. Throughout the long history of Israel, God tried to lead people to receive His grace by faith. God sent priests, prophets, and preachers to tell people how to believe. But the people still didn't get the message. It was like they had a cassette tape with the message "God loves you" on it, but they had no way to play it. They had hope, but they still had to wait and get ready. Finally, God sent His son, Jesus Christ, to show them His love. It's this coming, this *Advent* of Jesus we celebrate at Christmastime.

As we begin our journey toward Christmas today, let's remember why we celebrate. Jesus is the full and final proof of God's love. All of the hope of people in times past was fulfilled in Jesus. When the prophet Jeremiah wrote, "Behold, the days are coming, says the Lord, when I will fulfil the promise I made to the house of Israel and the house of Judah" (33:14), he was talking about Jesus. This promise was for Jesus to come.

Their hope has now become our faith. We know Jesus has come, and this we celebrate at Christmas. Thank God for the hope of people in the past. It gives us hope for living our days in order to know that God always keeps promises.

A Time of Giving

Text: Matthew 2:11, "Going into the house they saw the child with Mary his mother, and they fell down and worshiped him. Then, opening their treasures, they offered him gifts, gold and frankincense and myrrh."

Main Truth: Christmas is about giving God our worship.

Interest Object: A wrapped Christmas gift.

The Gospel of Matthew tells us about some wise men who went to see Baby Jesus not long after He was born. When they arrived where Jesus was, Matthew tells us, " they saw the child with Mary his mother, and they fell down and worshiped him. Then, opening their treasures, they offered him gifts."

Ever since Jesus was born and wise men came to worship Him by bringing gifts, Christmas has been a time of giving. We mainly give presents to one another, like this one I'm holding. I like that. I mean I like to give presents, and I enjoy receiving presents. At our house, there's a lot of whispering and paper rattling behind locked doors. It's exciting to give and receive, isn't it?

The one thing I don't want you to overlook, during our season of getting ready for Christmas, is that we need to worship God. We celebrate Christmas, because God gave Jesus as a baby in the manger. Jesus was perfect and without sin and gave His life to take away our sins. We need to believe in Jesus. Believing in Jesus means we worship Him, like the wise men did. Jesus deserves our love and faith.

As you prepare for Christmas, ask yourself, "What will I give to God?" Then answer, "I'll worship God. I'll sing, pray, praise God, and give my money to the Lord's work. I'll live for God and believe in Jesus as Savior and Lord." If you do that, you'll be receiving from Christmas what God wants to give you and giving to God what God wants from you. Christmas is about giving God our worship.

A Time of Seeking

Text: Matthew 2:1-12; Luke 2:1-20. Read this Scripture several times in your favorite version and summarize it for the children.

Main Truth: Anybody who honestly looks for Jesus will find Him and will find in Him just what they're looking for.

Last week I went to the mall to look for another Christmas present for my wife. I didn't know exactly what I was looking for, but I had to find something. I looked at clothes, housewares, jewelry, furniture, and electronics like clocks and televisions. I ended up seeing so many things that I didn't buy anything on that trip. You might say I just went seeking but not finding. Now I have a good idea of what I want to buy for her, so I'll have to go looking again. When you know what you're looking for, it makes the search easier.

Did you ever stop to think about how many people were seeking something or someone at the time Jesus was born? Mary and Joseph were seeking to do God's will. The shepherds were seeking the baby the angels told them about. The angels were seeking to praise God for sending Jesus. The wise men were seeking Jesus to worship Him. Herod was seeking to kill Baby Jesus. Everybody was seeking. Did anybody find what they were looking for?

I think they did. Anybody who honestly looks for Jesus will find Him, and they'll find in Him just what they're looking for. If you're looking for a friend, Jesus will be there. If you're seeking love, you can find it in Jesus. If you're wanting forgiveness, He'll give it to you. All our hopes, dreams, and faith are fulfilled in Jesus. You can find whatever you're looking for in life in Jesus!

Advent

A Time of Getting

Text: Luke 2:11, "To you is born this day in the city of David a Savior, who is Christ the Lord."

Main Truth: Jesus is God's great gift to all who believe.

Interest Object: An inexpensive gift for each child. I suggest a bookmark, piece of fruit, or Christmas candy.

I have a Christmas present for you this morning. I wanted to give you something, because I love you. Christmas is a time for giving, so I want you to have these Christmas bookmarks. I hope you'll use them. *(Distribute bookmarks.)*

Wait a minute! I just thought of something. I said Christmas is a time of giving. I'm doing all the giving, and you're just getting! God gives to us, too. In fact, the most beautiful truth of Christmas is what we've gotten from God.

Jesus is God's great gift to all who believe. We can hear this good news in Luke 2:11, when angels announced to shepherds what God was giving them, "To you is born this day in the city of David a Savior, who is Christ the Lord." Jesus wasn't given just to shepherds long ago but to all who believe in Him. Jesus was born to be our Savior, our Lord of life. When we believe in Jesus and receive Him as our own Savior, then He gives us God's gift of salvation forever. Jesus is God's great gift to all who believe. Merry Christmas to each of you!

2
Bible Study Week

How the Bible Helps Us

Text: Romans 15:4, "Whatever was written in former days was written for our instruction, that by steadfastness and by the encouragement of the scriptures we might have hope."

Main Truth: The Bible is our guide for daily living.

Interest Object: A picture of road signs or actual road signs, if you can obtain them legally.

When I was on vacation last summer, I noticed some road signs on the interstate highway that were new to me. *(Hold up pictures or signs.)* You'll recognize these road signs—stop, yield, speed limit, railroad crossing, and so forth. I saw all these, of course. But I also saw some new kinds of signs. One of them said "Food," and it showed me that there was a restaurant at the next exit. Another new sign said, "Hospital." I knew that if I needed a doctor, I could take that exit and find one. Other new signs showed me which motels were at exits or whether there were rest rooms at the rest stops. I found the new signs to be quite helpful and useful.

This week we're all studying the Bible. There will be a study for you, for youth, and for adults. We have some good leaders to teach us. Some of the things we'll learn are general—they apply to all of us and to a lot of areas of living. They're like the old kinds of road signs, with general information on them. Other things we'll learn are like the new road signs—specific truths we'll need right away and some not needed for awhile.

Whatever our needs right now, whether general or specific, the Bible is our guide for daily living. Romans 15:4 says, "Whatever was written in former days was written for our instruction, that by steadfastness and by the encouragement of the scriptures we might have hope." I hope you'll come to Bible study and learn how the Bible helps us.

3
Christmas

Understanding Jesus for Yourself

Text: Luke 2:1-14. Read this Scripture several times in your favorite version and summarize it for the children.

Main Truth: Each of us come to our own understanding of faith in Jesus.

Interest Object: A book of Christmas carols or a hymnal opened to the carol section.

Memory Maker: Sometimes booklets of Christmas carols are available from banks, insurance agencies, funeral homes, and so forth. Locate enough to give one to each child.

Merry Christmas! I know you know a lot of Christmas carols, like "Silent Night, Holy Night"; "The First Noel"; " Hark! the Herald Angels Sing"; and"Joy to the World." I want to tell you about another Christmas carol you probably don't know. First I want to read to you the Christmas story from Luke 2:1-14. *(Read text.)*

You know that Jesus was born in a stable. You know that He was wrapped in swaddling cloths, which were strips of cloth, and put in an animal feed box called a *manger*. But what if you had never heard these things about Jesus' birth? How would you explain Jesus' birth to people who knew nothing about it?

Well, that's exactly what the writer of the first American Christmas carol tried to do—explain Jesus' birth to people who knew nothing about it. The first American carol was written by a French Catholic missionary named John de Brebeuf in about 1640. He was a missionary to the Huron Indians in the Northeast. His Christmas carol was called, "Jesus Was Born." He sang of Jesus' birth by describing it like this:

> Within a lodge of broken bark
> The tender babe was found;
> A ragged robe of rabbit skin
> Enwrapped his beauty round;
> And as the hunter braves drew nigh
> The angel song rang loud and high;
> Jesus your king is born,
> Jesus is born,
> In excelsis gloria.

Now, we know that Jesus wasn't born in a bark lodge and wrapped in rabbit fur with Indian hunters who visited. But the missionary was explaining the birth of Jesus in a way the Huron Indians could understand and accept it for themselves.

Boys and girls, each of us has to come to our own understanding of faith in Jesus. You know the Christmas story from the Bible. When you believe in Jesus and receive Jesus in your own way for yourself, Christmas is a merry time indeed.

4
Christian Home Week

What Makes a House a Home?

Text: Luke 15:11-32. Read this Scripture several times in your favorite version and summarize it for the children.

Main Truth: God's love can't be lost or earned.

What makes a house a home? There's a difference between a house and a home. A *house* is a place, a building. But a *home* is a feeling of belonging, sense of togetherness, and spirit of love. It may be a place, but it's the feelings of the people in the place that are most important.

We can see this in a story Jesus told. It's about the prodigal son. In the story, a man had two sons. The younger of them asked his dad for the family money he'd receive at his dad's death. He then left home and spent it all. When he became desperate for help, he went home and found his father waiting to forgive and welcome him back home.

I think this story teaches us an important lesson: The home is a place of love. Home is where love is, and this love can't be lost, even when we wander away from home, act ugly, or do wrong. This love can't be earned, no matter how hard we try. It's given, not earned. Let's all give love in our homes and be thankful for the love we receive.

God's love can't be lost or earned. God loves us, because God is love. God loves us even when we don't appreciate it or act ugly to God or each other. I pray that God will give us happy homes and that we'll be thankful for God's love for us and our love for each other.

5
Church Music Week

We Have a Song to Sing!

Text: Colossians 3:16, "Sing psalms and hymns and spiritual songs with thankfulness in your hearts to God."

Main Truth: Music is an important part of our worship.

Interest Object: A musical instrument. I chose a violin because our minister of music played violin. You could use any instrument, including the church piano or organ.

This is Mr. Pylant's violin. I borrowed it from him this morning, because I want to play it for you. Although I've never had a lesson, I think I've figured out how to play it. I know you hold it under your chin like this, then you put the bow to the strings and slide the bow across the strings. If you want to play lower notes, you move your hand away from you. If you want to play higher notes, move it toward you. Let me try. I think I'll play, "Jesus Loves Me." *(Do it as best you can, which may not be very good.)*

That was awful! Maybe I need more practice! Mr. Pylant, please come play it like it's supposed to be played. *(He plays.)* That was beautiful. I guess you just have to know how.

I'm beginning to realize how important music is to our worship and how thankful I am for Mrs. Braswell at the organ, Miss Lanham at the piano, Mr. Pylant's singing and playing, the people in our choirs, and people who sing solos. I'm thankful to be a part of a singing church. I like our congregational hymns, responses, offertories, and other music.

Wow, music is an important part of our worship, isn't it? Maybe that's why Paul wrote in Colossians 3:16, "Sing psalms and hymns and spiritual songs with thankfulness in your hearts to God." Let's do this. We have a

27

song to sing! Let's sing about our love, gratitude, and praise to God. Let's express our thanks to those who are in our music program. Let's all take part in music every way we can through our church. I believe this will please God.

6
Deacon Election

Servants of the Lord

Text: 1 Timothy 3:13, "Those who serve well as deacons gain a good standing for themselves and also great confidence in the faith which is in Christ Jesus."

Main Truth: Deacons are servants of the Lord by serving God's people.

Interest Object: This will take some preparation. Locate a large piece of poster board. Cut it lengthwise into four equal strips. In the vertical and horizontal centers of the first strip, print in large block letters "Boss of the church." On the second, print "Paid worker." On the third, print "Doer of dirty jobs." On the fourth, print "Servant of the Lord." Now, use each strip and make them into hats by putting them around your head, marking the place for the right size, and gluing or stapling it together in the back. Now you're ready.

I want to talk to you about deacons. What is a deacon? If deacons wore hats with their job described on them, what would they say?

How about this one? *(Put on the hat that says "Boss of the church.")* Some people think deacons are kind of bosses of the church to tell the pastor, staff, and members what to do. However, in the New Testament we don't find that deacons were bosses of the church. Deacons aren't bosses of the church today either.

How about *paid workers*? *(Put on that hat.)* No, deacons aren't paid for their work. They do it for free. Deacons spend many hours working for the Lord and for the church. They do it without getting any money for it.

How about *doer of dirty jobs*? *(Change hats.)* Some people might think of deacons as people who do the dirty jobs of the church; jobs nobody else wants to do, like cleaning up dirty dishes, taking out garbage after church dinners, doing the yard work in the hot summertime, or painting Sunday School classrooms. But these aren't just jobs for deacons. Oh yes, some deacons help with these kinds of things, but it isn't their work for the Lord. Deacons aren't just doers of dirty jobs.

What are deacons, then? *(Put on the "Servant of the Lord" hat.)* This hat says, "Servant of the Lord." This is what the New Testament says deacons are. Deacons are servants of the Lord by serving God's people. They are servants, not bosses. They don't do it for money. They are to help people, not just do the dirty work.

You might say that deacons are pastor's helpers. They do the same kinds of things pastors do—meet people's needs, carry out the ministries and programs of the church, witness to people about Jesus, and visit people. Deacons are elected by the church to serve people by meeting needs. This is closest to the New Testament idea of what deacons are. First Timothy 3:13 says, "Those who *serve* well as deacons gain a good standing for themselves and also a great confidence in the faith which is in Christ Jesus" (author's italics).

7
Easter

A Symbol of Life

Text: Mark 16:1-7. Read this Scripture several times in your favorite version and summarize it for the children.

Main Truth: Jesus was dead but came back to life!

Interest Object: A monarch butterfly or picture of one. Actually, any kind of butterfly could be used.

This is a monarch butterfly. You'll see a lot of them in the spring. It wasn't always a beautiful butterfly. It changed. It used to be a caterpillar. Then one day, it climbed onto a branch of a tree somewhere and spun a web around itself which is called a *cocoon*. It stayed in this cocoon like it was dead; until one day it came out, changed from an caterpillar into a beautiful butterfly.

From the early days of Christianity, the butterfly has been a symbol of life at Easter. Now, obviously Jesus wasn't a caterpillar who changed into a butterfly, but something like this did happen to Jesus. We read about it in Mark 16:1-7. *(Read text.)*

Jesus was dead but came back to life! That's why we celebrate Easter. Jesus died on the cross and arose the first Easter morning.

I'm glad we can celebrate the resurrection of Jesus. Let's thank God that Jesus, who died, came back to life!

8
Epiphany Sunday

Finding What You're Looking For

Text: Matthew 6:33, "Seek first his kingdom and his righteousness, and all these things shall be yours as well."

Main Truth: If we always seek to put God first in life, God will take care of us.

    I wonder if you can help me this morning. I've lost something and need to find it. I came in here earlier with my candy jar and put it down somewhere. I don't remember where, but I'm sure it's nearby. Would you look around for it?
    Oh, you found it. Thank you. Since you helped me find it, why don't we each take a piece? *(Pass it around quickly.)*
    Today is the day many churches celebrate the time when the wise men arrived at the place where they worshiped Baby Jesus. They were looking for Him, and when they found Him, they worshiped Him and gave Him presents. Their search reminds us that when we truly seek the Lord, we will always find Him.
    One of my favorite verses in the Bible is Matthew 6:33. It says, "Seek first his kingdom and his righteousness, and all these things shall be yours as well." I think this verse means that if we always seek to put God first in life, God will take care of us. My prayer for each of us is that we'll do this; put God first, knowing that when we do we'll find all the happiness, love, and other things of life we'll need.

9
Father's Day

How to Honor Your Father

Text: Genesis 45:3, " 'I am Joseph; is my father still alive?' "

Main Truth: God wants us to honor our fathers every day with love, respect, and obedience.

A long time ago in Bible days, there was a large family. The father in this family was named Jacob. He had twelve sons. Before the youngest son was born, the eleventh son, Joseph, made his ten older brothers mad at him. The brothers were so mad they wanted to kill Joseph. Instead of killing him, they sold him to a some travelers as a slave. They told their father a wild animal had killed him. They didn't think they would ever see Joseph again. And they didn't for many years.

During those years when they didn't see Joseph, he grew up to become not a slave but a rich and powerful man in Egypt, where he lived. In fact, he became governor of Egypt. When the ten brothers had to go to Egypt to buy food, they went before Joseph. He recognized them, but they didn't recognize him. Joseph sent the ten brothers home to bring the younger brother.

When they returned, Joseph told them he was the brother they had sold into slavery long ago. They were shocked and afraid, but he forgave them. Do you know the first thing Joseph asked them after he told them who he was? He said, ' "I am Joseph; is my father still alive?' " Imagine not knowing for years and years whether or not your father was alive, much less getting to honor him on Father's Day! Joseph brought his father and his whole family to Egypt and cared for them.

Today is the day we honor our fathers. Joseph's example and the Bible teaches us to honor our fathers and our mothers. We're doing what the Bible teaches when we honor our parents. I don't think the Bible meant for us to honor our fathers just one day of the year. God wants us to honor our fathers every day with love, respect, and obedience. Today, put your arms around you father's neck and tell him you love him. Then every day, honor him with your love and obedience. You'll both be glad you did!

10
Foreign Missions Sunday

Little Things Are Important, Too!

Text: Mark 4:30-32, "He said, 'With what can we compare the kingdom of God, or what parable shall we use for it? It is like a grain of mustard seed, which, when sown upon the ground, is the smallest of all the seeds on earth; yet when it is sown it grows up and becomes the greatest of all shrubs, and puts forth large branches, so that the birds of the air can make nests in its shade.' "

Main Truth: Every prayer and gift for missions is important, no matter how small!

Interest Object: A tire stem. You can locate an old one or new one from a service station, tire dealer, or auto garage.

Last month, I bought two new tires for my car. I wanted good safe tires for my car. I paid almost $100 for each tire. I felt really safe after buying such good new tires.

About a week after I bought my new tires, I went out to get in my car, and one tire was flat. It was one of the new tires, too! Boy, was I upset. I took it off and went back to the dealer. He put some air into it and tried to find out why it went flat. There was nothing wrong with the tire! The reason it went flat was because when I put on new tires, I didn't think to put on new stems.

This is a tire stem. It costs about fifty cents! I paid a lot of money for a new tire, and a tire stem that cost very little caused the flat. I learned from this that little things are important, too!

The same thing is true in missions. We have a huge world to reach with the good news of Jesus Christ. Does what I do or what you do make a difference? You see, maybe you and I can't give a lot of money to missions, and maybe we think one person praying won't do much. But I want to remind you that our money and prayers join the money and prayers of thousands of other people around the world. Together we make a lot of difference. Every prayer and gift for missions is important, no matter how small! Jesus once compared His kingdom to a mustard seed. It starts out small but grows into something big. One person praying about and giving money to missions is small but gets larger when it is put with what others do. We must each do our part, no matter how small.

11
Good Friday

Who Is Good Friday Good For?

Text: 1 Corinthians 15:3-4, "I delivered to you as of first importance what I also received, that Christ died for our sins in accordance with the scriptures, that he was buried, that he was raised on the third day in accordance with the scriptures."

Main Truth: Good Friday is good for all, especially those who believe Jesus is our Savior!

Today is called Good Friday in churches throughout the world. Did you ever wonder why it's called this? I mean, who is Good Friday good for?
It wasn't good for Jesus. He died. Yes, He died willingly, but it was still painful. It wasn't good for the disciples. All their hope and faith were in Jesus, and now He was dead. It must have been a terrible day for them.
It wasn't a good day for Mary, Jesus' mother, or the other women at the cross. It wasn't a good day for any of Jesus' family or friends. It wasn't a good day for Jesus' enemies, because their troubles with Him were over only for a few days. So who was Good Friday good for?
Good Friday is good for you and me, because in Jesus' dying we have the possibility of being saved from our sins. If Jesus hadn't died and been raised again, we would still be lost in our own sinfulness. But because Jesus was sinless and died on the cross, our sins are paid for, and we can be forgiven. Good Friday is good for all who believe Jesus is Savior! Thank God for what Jesus did on Good Friday.

12
Graduation Sunday

An Important Step in Life

Text: Ecclesiastes 11:9, "Rejoice, . . . in your youth, and let your heart cheer you in the days of your youth; walk in the ways of your heart and the sight of your eyes."

Main Truth: Graduation is an important step in life and should be celebrated.

Interest Object: An academic cap with tassel.

This is my son's hat that he will wear to his high school graduation this afternoon. It's kind of funny looking, don't you think? People have been wearing these for hundreds of years. They're called *mortarboards*; I guess because they're flat and square, like boards you'd carry mortar or cement on. Attached to the hat is a tassel. The tassel has also been worn at graduation for a long time. You could say these are symbols of graduation. The tassel is especially so. When the graduates march into the auditorium this afternoon their tassels will all be hanging from the right side of their hats. After they receive their diplomas, the principal will say they are officially graduated from high school. At that time, the graduates will reach up and move their tassels from the right side of their hats to the left side. It's something nearly all graduates do to show they've graduated and things are different for them. It's a little thing to demonstrate a big event that's happened to them. Graduation from high school or college is an important step in life and should be celebrated.

Today, in our worship service, we honor our graduates. I will call each of them forward and give them a gift from the church. It's our way of letting them know we're proud of them, love them, and wish them well in whatever they do. Whenever you graduate, we'll do the same for you. Graduation is an important step in life and should be celebrated. As Ecclesiastes 11:9 says, "Rejoice, . . . in your youth, and let your heart cheer you in the days of your youth; walk in the ways of your heart and the sight of your eyes." It's a call to celebrate life while you're young. Life isn't always so happy, and celebration is important whenever there's reason to celebrate.

13

Home Missions Sunday

Putting on Our "Jesus Glasses"

Text: Matthew 9:36, "When he saw the crowds, he had compassion for them, because they were harassed and helpless, like sheep without a shepherd."

Main Truth: We must see people like Jesus saw them—through love.

Interest Object: A pair of dark sunglasses.

When Jesus looked at people, He saw everyone the same way—with eyes of love. He didn't see good people or bad people, tall or short people, fat or skinny people, rich or poor people. He saw people who needed God's love, and He was always willing to give them this love. Matthew 9:36 says about Jesus, "When he saw the crowds, he had compassion for them, because they were harassed and helpless, like sheep without a shepherd." This verse tells us how Jesus saw people. "He had compassion for them" means He loved them and cared about them. "Harassed and helpless" means they were needy and had no one else to turn to. "Sheep without a shepherd" would wander around helplessly, until they became lost and would probably die. Jesus knew He had to reach these people with the good news of God's love.

We, too, need to tell people the good news of God's love. But before we can do this, we need to see people and their needs. I know you see people every day. However, we need to see people like Jesus saw them—through love.

This is just an ordinary pair of sunglasses. I wish somehow I could turn them into what I would call "Jesus glasses." If I could do that, whenever I put on my "Jesus glasses," I would automatically see people through love like Jesus did. I wouldn't see the color of their skin, whether they were rich or poor, how they were dressed, or how they looked. I would just see people—needy, hurting, and broken, like sheep without a shepherd needing God's love and my love.

However, there's no such thing as "Jesus glasses." So we have to think and try hard to see people like Jesus did. He saw the need and did something about it. We must see the needs and tell everyone what He did. That's part of God's plan for the church—see the needs and tell people Jesus is the answer to their needs.

Today is home missions Sunday. This week, be a missionary in your home, school, and neighborhood. Pray for all our missionaries in America each day this week. Give as much money as you can to help missionaries tell people about Jesus. If we'll do those three things, we'll be helping people for Jesus.

14
Labor Day

Be the Best Worker You Can Be

Text: Genesis 2:15, "The Lord God took the man and put him in the garden of Eden to till it and keep it."

Main Truth: We are meant to work.

I'm sure you've heard the story of Adam and Eve in the garden of Eden. God created Adam and Eve as the first man and woman in the world. Does anybody know what Adam's job was? What work did Adam do? *(Let them try to answer.)*

Adam was a gardener. God gave him that job. Genesis 2:15 says, "The Lord God took the man and put him in the garden of Eden to till it and keep it." This means God means for us to work. God didn't intend for Adam to sit in the garden doing nothing but eating and sleeping. God wanted him to work, so Adam became a gardener.

Tomorrow is Labor Day, a day to honor people who work. We celebrate this holiday by resting a day or receiving a day off from work.

Boys and girls, I want you to decide now to work hard at whatever you do. Right now your job is to learn. That isn't so easy sometimes, so you have to work hard at learning good thoughts, habits, and behavior.

I'm sure all of you have jobs to do around the house—picking up your toys, doing dishes, taking care of pets, or taking out the garbage. Do the best you can at whatever you're asked to do. You will be proud of your work, and your parents will be pleased.

Some of you are in school. Work at being the best student you can be. Do the best you can and put forth your best effort. Work hard at your studies so that you can be proud of yourself.

Later in life, you will work at a job. Find something you enjoy doing and do your best.

We were meant to work. Be the best worker you can be in whatever you do.

15

Lent (Preparation for Easter)

The Hand of Love

Text: Galatians 6:11, "See with what large letters I am writing to you with my own hand."

Main Truth: Writing is one way to express our love and appreciation to others.

For the next six weeks we're going to be preparing to celebrate Easter. Each week of this preparation time I'm going to ask you to do something that will help you think about God, other people, or yourself in a special way.

A lot of what we know about God and Jesus is written in the Bible. We might say that the Bible is God's love letter to us. It tells us of God's love.

But, you know, somebody had to sit down and write the words we know as our Bible. Verses like Galatians 6:11 says, "See with what large letters I am writing to you with my own hand." These are the words of Paul. He usually had someone else to do the actual writing, but in this verse he wrote the letters himself.

Just as Paul and others wrote long ago, I want you to write someone this week. Writing is one way to express our love and appreciation to others. Write a letter, or if you can't write yet, draw a picture this week and send it to someone you love. This is a way of saying "I love you" or "I think about you." It may be someone far away or someone close by. Let them know you are thankful for them. You'll be glad you did. Begin to think about some special people and what they mean to you. It's a way to get ready for Easter.

The Voice of Love

Text: Proverbs 16:24, "Pleasant words are like a honeycomb, sweetness to the soul and health to the body."

Main Truth: We can give joy to others through words of love and kindness.

Interest Object: A telephone or toy telephone.

Did you write somebody a letter or draw a picture last week? This week I want you to call someone on the telephone and say, "I love you," "I'm sorry," "Thank you," or whatever you feel like you need to say to some special person.

Usually when I use a telephone like this one, it's for business to receive or give information or to check on something or someone. Why not use the telephone to make someone happier? Why not call someone for no other reason than to say, "I love you"? I imagine your grandmother, mom, dad, brother, sister, friend, or teacher at church would like to receive a call like that. I know I would. Wouldn't you?

We can give joy to others by words of love and kindness. Proverbs 16:24 says, "Pleasant words are like a honeycomb, sweetness to the soul and health to the body." I hope you'll call someone this week and say words of love to them.

The Gift of Love

Text: Philippians 4:17, "Not that I seek the gift; but I seek the fruit which increases to your credit."

Main Truth: Giving to others is one way to demonstrate our love for them.

Interest Object: A gift you have received from someone that was especially made for you or given to you for no reason except that someone loves you.

This is the first piece on needlework my daughter De Ann ever did. When she was about six or seven years old, she wanted to learn to do needlepoint. Her mother agreed to teach her. Rather than using a pattern someone else had designed, she designed her own. She knew what she wanted it to say.

Can you read it? It says, "I love dad." After she created it, she gave it to me. I proudly display it on the wall in my office. It means a great deal to me. Boys and girls, giving to others is one way to demonstrate our love for them. It isn't the only way, but it's a good way! Paul found this out when he received a gift of money from the people of the church at Philippi. He loved this church, and they loved him. They helped him by praying for him and sending him money. He wrote a letter to thank them for their gift. In it he said something important. He wrote, "Not that I seek the gift; but I seek the fruit which increases to your credit" (Phil. 4:17). In other words, Paul said that when they gave him the gift, they were as blessed for the giving as he was for receiving!

I believe that's still true. When we give to someone, we are blessed. As you continue to prepare for Easter, I want you to give a gift to someone this week, somebody who means a lot to you, but to whom you don't express your love often. Make something like a picture, needlepoint, or cookies. Buy a plant, scarf, or something and give it to somebody special. Just be sure you give it out of love.

The Prayer of Love

Text: Ephesians 6:18, "Pray on every occasion, as the Spirit leads. For this reason keep alert and never give up; pray always for all God's people" (GNB).

Main Truth: Praying for one another is one of the most important things we can do.

Interest Object: A pair of crutches.

This is a pair of crutches. My son had to use them several years ago, when he had knee surgery from a football injury. Since we bought them, we decided to keep them after he didn't need them anymore. It's a good thing we did. There have been several times since that we have loaned them to a friend who needed them for awhile.

There are times in life when we need a little extra help. That's when crutches come in handy. There are other ways, too, in which we need help from other people. In fact, there are a lot of things in life we couldn't or shouldn't do alone. It's good to have help when you need it.

One way to help other people is to pray for them. Praying for one another is one of the most important things we can do. Ephesians 6:18 reminds us, "Pray on every occasion, as the Spirit leads. For this reason keep alert and never give up; pray always for all God's people."

This week I want you to make a list of ten people to pray for each day. Have someone help you make the list, if you need to. Put on the list the names of friends, family members, even people you don't like very well. Then, each day, pray for everyone on the list. This is one of the best things you can do for others.

The Mind of Love

Text: Philippians 4:6, "Don't worry about anything, but in all your prayers ask God for what you need, always asking him with a thankful heart" (GNB).

Main Truth: Prayer brings peace of mind that money can't buy.

Interest Object: A dollar bill.

Can you name some things this dollar bill *can* buy? *(Let them name some.)* That's right! Now, can you name some things this dollar *can't* buy? (Let them try.) That's good. Now I want to tell you about something I know this dollar can't buy. It's called peace of mind. That means a good, quiet feeling within yourself that makes you happy with who you are. Money can't buy that. I want to tell you how you can have it.

Prayer brings peace of mind that money can't buy. When we talk to God about our problems, needs, fears, and hopes, we have a good feeling within ourselves. That's peace of mind. It means we don't worry about things and people; we just talk to God about it and trust that they will be OK.

I think this is what Philippians 4:6 means when it says, "Don't worry about anything, but in all your prayers ask God for what you need, always asking him with a thankful heart."

This week, boys and girls, I want you to spend some time each day talking to God about yourself. Tell God what you're thankful for, what you think about, what bothers you, and what you've done wrong and need God to forgive you of. I believe this will help get you ready for Easter.

The Joy of Love

Text: Philippians 4:4, "Rejoice in the Lord always; again I will say, Rejoice."

Main Truth: Because Jesus is Lord, we can live with a sense of joy.

Spring is a beautiful season in the year. Flowers are blooming, days are warming, the sun is shining, and warm rains water trees and grass. I think it's good that Easter is during the springtime. We have a lot to be happy about.

Another word for happiness is joy. This week I want you to let your joy grow as we come closer to Easter, a day of special joy in our faith. How? I'm glad you asked.

Do some things this week that bring you joy and make you feel good and happy. Invite a friend over to your house to play, eat with you, or spend the night (with your parent's permission, of course). Go outside in the sunshine instead of staying in and watching TV. Visit someone you enjoy being with. Treat yourself to something special. You can think of something that gives you joy. Do it this week.

Doing this will help us get ready for Easter Sunday, and we'll be doing what Philippians 4:4 says, "Rejoice in the Lord always; again I will say, Rejoice." Because Jesus is Lord, we can live with a sense of joy!

16
Lord's Supper

A Timeless Reminder

Text: 1 Corinthians 11:23-26, "I received from the Lord what I also delivered to you, that the Lord Jesus on the night when he was betrayed took bread, and when he had given thanks, he broke it, and said, 'This is my body which is for you. Do this in remembrance of me.' In the same way also the cup, after supper, saying, 'This cup is the new covenant in my blood. Do this, as often as you drink it, in remembrance of Me.' For as often as you eat this bread and drink the cup, you proclaim the Lord's death until he comes."

Main Truth: The Lord's Supper is a reminder of the past, present, and future.

Interest Object: A high school graduation ring.

This is my daughter's high school graduation ring. She just got it. Some of you know De Ann is in the eleventh grade, a junior in high school. That means she has the rest of this year and all of next year before she graduates. Those who buy high school rings receive them in their junior year. I guess this is so they'll have something to look forward to. They can wear their rings almost a whole year, looking ahead toward graduation.

After graduation, the rings will help the graduate think back and remember teachers, friends, good times, and laughs they had in high school. A graduation ring is a reminder of the past, too.

Some high school graduates will go to college. When they graduate from college, some will buy college graduation rings. So the new rings will have new meaning for them at that time. This ring is in some ways a reminder of the past, present, and future.

The Lord's Supper is also a reminder of the past, present, and future. It reminds us of who Jesus was and what He did in the past. The bread reminds us of Jesus' body which was put on the cross for our sins. It reminds us that Jesus died for us. The cup reminds us of the same thing—that Jesus died by shedding His blood to forgive us of our sins. This is what 1 Corinthians 11:24-25 means when it quotes Jesus as saying, " 'Do this in remembrance of me.' " That's talking about the past meaning of the Lord's Supper. We remember Jesus through it.

The Lord's Supper also has meaning for now, the present time we live in. It tells us that God is with us today. It's a symbol. A *symbol* is something that stands for something else. A graduation ring is a symbol that someone has graduated or is about to graduate. The Lord's Supper is a symbol. Jesus talked about a "new covenant" in 1 Corinthians 11:25. This means a new way of relating to God. The Lord's Supper is a reminder of Jesus' spiritual presence in the world today.

The Lord's Supper also has a future meaning. Paul wrote, "For as often as you eat this bread and drink the cup, you proclaim the Lord's death until he comes" (1 Cor. 11:26). The last three words, "until he comes," are a promise that Jesus will return to Earth some day. So, when we have the Lord's Supper, we remember that Jesus is indeed coming again—the promise for the future.

As we observe the Lord's Supper today, remember who Jesus was and what He did, that He's present with us today in Spirit and He's coming again in the future. All these meanings are found in the Lord's Supper.

Has Everyone Been Served?

Text: Matthew 26:26-28, "Now as they were eating, Jesus took bread, and blessed, and broke it, and gave it to the disciples and said, 'Take, eat; this is my body.' And he took a cup, and when he had given thanks he gave it to them, saying, 'Drink of it, all of you; for this is my blood of the covenant, which is poured out for many for the forgiveness of sins.' "

Main Truth: We need to tell others about who Jesus was and what He did for them.

Interest Object: Communion bread and cup. Hold each up as you talk about it.

Not long ago, I was in a worship service where the Lord's Supper was being served. After the bread was given to everyone, the pastor said, " 'Take, eat, this is my body' " (Matt. 26:26). Everyone ate their bread. Then they served the cup to us. I fully expected the pastor to say the words we usually hear just before we drank from the cup: " 'Drink of it, all of you; for this is my blood of the covenant, which is poured out for the forgiveness of sins' " (Matt. 26:27-28). But, to my surprise, instead of the regular words for the cup, the pastor asked in a loud voice, "Has everyone been served?" Then he looked around the room for a moment. I felt a little bit uncomfortable, thinking maybe somebody had been missed. Then the pastor said, "No, everyone hasn't been served. There are millions of people out there in the world who haven't been served because they don't know about the love of Jesus represented in this cup. Go, tell everyone you meet that God loves them and Jesus died for their sins to be forgiven. Let us remember this as we drink this cup."

Boys and girls, as we celebrate the Lord's Supper today, let's remember the meaning it has for us, that Jesus is our Savior. Let's also remember the message of the Lord's Supper, that God loves all people and offers salvation through Jesus Christ. We need to tell others who Jesus was and what He did for them and everybody.

A Strange Time for Singing

Text: Mark 14:26, "When they had sung a hymn, they went out to the Mount of Olives."

Main Truth: We can celebrate our love for Jesus even in those times when we don't feel like celebrating.

Did you ever have a time when you were supposed to be happy and celebrate, but you weren't happy and didn't feel like celebrating? If you haven't, you will at some time in the future, because life isn't always happy.

The disciples must have had such a strange feeling that night in the upper room when Jesus gave them the Lord's Supper for the first time. They had been together for three years. That night Jesus told them that one of them was a traitor who would betray Him, they were all going to leave Him, and He was going to die. Then He gave them the bread and cup of the Lord's

Supper as a symbol of what would happen to Him. After that, Mark 14:26 tells us, "When they had sung a hymn, they went out to the Mount of Olives."

I suppose there never was a time when they felt less like singing than then. Yet they sang. Why? What did they have to sing about at such a time as that? I think the disciples' singing was a celebration of their relationship with Jesus. I believe singing lifted their spirits and reminded them of God's love for them, which was given through Jesus.

We can learn from them. We can celebrate our love for Jesus, even in those times when we don't feel like celebrating. Maybe if we do sing, even when we don't feel like it, the singing will make us feel better and give us joy, even in a time of sadness. In Jesus, we can sing at times when we have unhappy or sad feelings.

Do You See a Reflection?

Text: 1 Corinthians 11:23-25, "The Lord Jesus on the night when he was betrayed took bread, and when he had given thanks, he broke it, and said, 'This is my body which is for you. Do this in remembrance of me.' In the same way also the cup, after supper, saying, 'This cup is the new covenant in my blood. Do this, as often as you drink it, in remembrance of me.'"

Main Truth: In the Lord's Supper we can clearly see what Jesus has done for us.

Interest Object: Two mirrors—one clear and clean and the other smeared so that the reflection is unclear.

Do you know what a reflection is? A reflection is when you see something in something else. When you look at a lake and see the trees on the other side, as if they're upside down at the water's edge, you are seeing a reflection. Or when you look at yourself in a mirror, you see your reflection.

I brought two mirrors with me today. They look just alike from the back. But look at the front, where the mirror is. If you were combing your hair and needed to look at yourself in a mirror, would you use this one *(hold out the smudged one)* or this one *(hold out the other one)*. Yeah, I would too. Because when you need a reflection, you want it to be as clear as it can be.

The Lord's Supper is, in a way, a reflection of Jesus. We don't see His face

Lord's Supper

in it, like we would ours in a mirror, but He gave it to us as a way to remember Him. Another way to say *remember* is to say reflect. The Lord's Supper helps us remember who Jesus was—our Lord and Savior—and what Jesus did—gave His body and blood for us. Listen to what Paul wrote about the Lord's Supper. *(Read text, accentuating the words* me *and* remembrance.*)* I think Jesus wanted His followers to see Him in the Lord's Supper.

As you watch your parents take the Lord's Supper today, or as you take it, think of Jesus. Remember what He did and why He did it. Jesus loves you. Remember this when you see the Lord's Supper.

17

Maundy Thursday

How Love Is Measured

Text: John 13:1-5,14-15. Read this Scripture several times in your favorite version and summarize it for the children.

Main Truth: Love is measured by our service to one another.

Interest Object: A small towel.

Memory Maker: A small towel or washcloth for each child. Inexpensive ones are available at discount stores or factory outlets. Even a paper towel could suffice.

We measure age in years. We measure size in feet and inches. We measure distance in yards and miles. We measure speed in miles per hour. But how do we measure love? There's no way, you say? We could say that love is measured by our service to one another. Jesus taught this on the night He began the Lord's Supper, a night long ago.

Jesus and the disciples were in an upper room eating supper together. While they were eating, Jesus did something surprising to the disciples. He got up from the table, tied a towel around His waist, poured water into a large bowl, and began to wash the disciples' feet. It was an example of loving service. Jesus was doing the job of a servant. After He had washed all the disciples' feet, He told them that they ought to be willing to do the same for each other. He meant that they ought to serve one another willingly, like He had served them. He did it as an act of love and humility.

This is an important lesson for us. If we love each other, we'll be willing to do things for each other. Love is measured by our service to one another.

Nobody should act like a big shot, and nobody should act like a nobody. We should all serve each other in love, like Jesus did.

I have a friend who likes to say, "There's a towel with your name on it." He means that there's a job for everyone who is willing to serve the Lord by serving other people. I want each of you to have one of these towels. Let it remind you what Jesus did on this night long ago. Let it also remind us to be loving servants of one another, because love is measured by humble service.

18
Memorial Day

A Different Beatitude

Text: Revelation 14:13, "I heard a voice from heaven saying, 'Write this: Blessed are the dead who die in the Lord henceforth.' 'Blessed indeed,' says the Spirit, 'that they may rest from their labors, for their deeds follow them!' "

Main Truth: It's good to remember and honor loved ones who have died.

Some of you know about the Beatitudes. The Beatitudes are those sayings of Jesus found in Matthew 5. Some of you learned about them in Sunday School or Vacation Bible School. They all start with the same word—*blessed. Blessed* means happy. Jesus said blessed are the poor in spirit, those who mourn, the meek, those who hunger and thirst after righteousness, and so on. Well, today I want to tell you about a beatitude Jesus didn't say. I call it "A Different Beatitude." It's different because of what it talks about—death. We usually don't think about death and happiness together. This beatitude is found in the last book of the Bible, Revelation 14:13. It says, " 'Blessed are the dead who die in the Lord.' " The same verse quotes God's Spirit as saying, " 'Blessed indeed, . . . that they may rest from their labors, for their deeds follow them!' "

This is a great verse, because it teaches us that people who die as Christians are happy, even though we might be sad. They are at rest, and we should remember what they did while they were alive. In fact, that's what this weekend is all about.

This is the weekend we remember the people who have died in service to our country. Many people have fought in wars so America can be free. Some of them died doing this. We honor them on Memorial Day.

It's good to remember and honor our loved ones who have died. Not only people who died for the country, but people in our families, church, and town who have died. When you think about them, remember what the different beatitude teaches us.

19
Mother's Day

Mothers Know Best

Text: Proverbs 31:28, "Her children rise up and call her blessed."

Main Truth: Thank God for mothers who know and do what's best for us.

Today is Mother's Day. I know we all love our mothers even when we don't like what they do, such as make us eat healthy food instead of junk food, go to school when we'd rather play or watch TV, take piano lessons, or do chores. Mothers know what's best for us and make us do it, even when we don't appreciate it at the time.

Today I want you to put your arms around your mother's neck and thank her for caring enough about you to guide you. Thank God for mothers who know and do what's best for us! You'll be doing what the Bible teaches us to do in Proverbs 31:28, "Her children rise up and call her blessed." Thank your mother for being your mother and for doing what mothers are supposed to do. Thank God for your mother.

20
New Year's Sunday

What to Lose and What to Seek

Text: 1 Peter 2:1-2, "Put away all malice and all guile and insincerity and envy and all slander. Like newborn babes, long for the pure spiritual milk, that by it you may grow up to salvation."

Main Truth: We must get rid of our bad attitudes and seek to grow up in the Lord.

Interest Object: A small sign saying, "Closed for inventory." You might have a local merchant loan you one, or you can print your own on poster board.

Have you seen a sign like this at any businesses in town? It says, "Closed for inventory." This is the time of year for stores to count what they sold in the past year. In this way, they can see what didn't sell and know what not to order again. By taking inventory, they learn what to pay taxes on and the value of their current merchandise. Sometimes they even close for a day or two to take inventory.

It might not be a bad idea for us to do the same thing in our own lives on this first Sunday of the new year. It's a good time to look at our own attitudes over the past year to see what we need to get rid of, look ahead to the new year, and decide how to make it a better year than we've ever had. It's time to take a personal inventory, to take stock of what to lose and what to seek in the new year.

We need some help to do this. I suggest 1 Peter 2:1-2 to guide us. It says, "Put away all malice and all guile and insincerity and envy and all slander. Like newborn babes, long for the pure spiritual milk, that by it you may grow up to salvation." This teaches us that we must get rid of our bad attitudes and seek to grow up in the Lord. We must lose any bad thoughts we have about other people, trying to deceive people by lying to them, wanting what others have, and talking badly about others. We must seek to grow in grace and kindness and faith and all the other things that make us better people in the Lord.

This is a new year. Let's live in it better than we ever have before. Get rid of the bad habits, and develop good habits. If we do this, then we can have a happy new year!

21
Old Year's Sunday

Old and New—Side by Side

Text: Psalm 90:12, "Teach us to number our days that we may get a heart of wisdom."

Main truth: In each day we should seek to live wisely and well, pleasing God in all we do.

When I drive from my home in North Carolina to my mother's home in Virginia, I usually take some shortcuts over some back roads. I've noticed a strange sight when I go one particular way. I want to tell you about that sight.

On a country road there's a place where another country road crosses. There's a sign showing an intersection ahead, but the place has no name. It's just a crossroads—no town or anything. If you look to your right at this crossroads, you'll see two houses on the same lot. One is exactly in front of the other. The house in the back is old, made of wood, needs painting, and doesn't look lived in. The house in the front, not more than a few feet away, is brand new and made of brick. This house looks lived in I've often wondered about those two houses, the old and the new—side by side. Why would anyone build houses so close together? Why didn't they tear the old one down before or after they built the new one?

I don't know the answers to my questions, but I have some guesses. I think the same family probably owns both houses. I think they lived in the old house for a long time, maybe even a very long time. I can imagine babies were born to this family, while they lived in this old house, and maybe some older family members even died in it. So, when it came time to build a new house, they wanted to keep the old one around for memory's sake. They built the new one in front of the old one, but the old one is always right behind them, reminding them of the past. I think that's kind of interesting, don't you?

Today is a little bit like the two houses I just told you about. We call the Sunday between Christmas and New Year's, "Old Year's Sunday." It's like living in an old year, one that's just about to pass forever and full of good and bad memories, and a new year, full of promises and potential. We're between the old and the new—side by side. So, how do we live in these days?

There's a verse of Scripture that says, "Teach us to number our days that we may get a heart of wisdom" (Ps. 90:12). This means that each day is important, each day past and each new day. In each day we should seek to live wisely, pleasing God in all we do. Learn from the past, put our whole selves into the present, and be hopeful for the future. If we do this, both the old year and the new will have meaning to us—side by side.

22
Palm Sunday

A Parade for Jesus

Text: Matthew 21:1-11. Read this Scripture several times in your favorite version and summarize it for the children.

Main Truth: Jesus wants us to accept Him as the King of Love.

Interest Object: Palm fronds. Since most of us live where these aren't readily available, I suggest making them out of green construction paper.

Memory Maker: A palm frond for each child.

Everybody loves a parade! My favorite is the Macy's Thanksgiving Day parade with the big balloons. My wife's favorite is the Rose Parade with the big floats decorated with flowers. There have been a lot of parades in the past for heroes, special visitors, returned astronauts, and local people who did well in some way. But this parade for Jesus took place on this day long ago. It was Jesus' triumphal entry into Jerusalem, and we read about it in Matthew 21:1-11. *(Read text.)*

This parade was Jesus' last public invitation to accept Him as the King of Love. What made it strange was that rather than Jesus being happy about it, He wept during it. He cried. I believed He cried because He knew the people who were cheering and waving palm branches, like these, hadn't really accepted Him as the King of Love and would soon want Him to die. As we read about the other events of Holy Week, we find Jesus was right. Those who called out "Hosanna!" on Sunday were the same ones who called for Him to be killed later in the same week. They hadn't really understood who He was.

We know who Jesus is. Jesus wants us to accept Him as the King of Love. He proved His love for us by coming, living, dying, and rising again. Believe in Jesus, live for Jesus, and tell others about Jesus' love. When we do these things, we prove that Jesus is the King of Love to us!

23
Pentecost Sunday

The Birthday of the Church

Text: Acts 2:1,4, "When the day of Pentecost had come, they were all together in one place. . . . And they were all filled with the Holy Spirit . . ."

Main Truth: God's presence in our lives gives us spiritual power.

Interest Object: A birthday cake or picture of one.

Memory Maker: How about giving a cupcake with a candle on it to each child after the service? Have a Sunday School class or department make these for you or someone who enjoys baking. Many people are anxious for some way to participate. This is a one way to involve others.

You know what this is. It's a birthday cake. I brought it to church because today is a birthday, not for a person but for the church. Today is Pentecost Sunday, a day to celebrate the time in early church history when God came in the person of the Holy Spirit. We read about it in Acts 2:1,4. "When the day of Pentecost had come, they were all together in one place. . . . And they were all filled with the Holy Spirit . . ." This verse is talking about the people who believed in and followed Jesus, soon to be called Christians. They were meeting in a large room when they heard a sound like wind and saw what looked like fire, and God's Spirit filled them with a new sense of His presence and power. This experience was known as Pentecost. I want to help you understand it.

I think a good way to understand what was happening is to think of it as the birthday of the church. With the coming of the Holy Spirit into the world, the time of the Christian church really began. This is what Pentecost is all about—the coming of God to people in a fresh new way. God's presence was known by the symbols of wind and fire. This presence gave them power, spiritual power.

God's presence in our lives gives us spiritual power. This is why we celebrate Pentecost Sunday today. We don't need to seek to repeat the signs and symbols of God's coming in the person of the Holy Spirit. This was a unique experience for the early believers. What we do need is the power it symbolizes. It's still available to us. We find it by receiving Jesus into our lives. When we fully accept Jesus and realize God is with us, then we know the power of God's presence, just like those present at Pentecost, the birthday of the church!

24
Race Relations Sunday

Outside, Inside, and All Over

Text: Acts 10:28, "God has shown me that I should not call any man common or unclean."

Main Truth: God accepts every person equally, and so should we.

Interest Object: Three cups—one fancy, pretty, and clean on the outside but with chocolate smeared on the inside to make it look dirty; one nice, white, ordinary cup, but not too fancy, dirty on the outside but clean on the inside; one old mug or cup, not-too-nice looking but clean inside and outside.

If I offered you a drink from one of these cups, I think I know which one most of you would pick. You'd want to drink from this beautiful china cup. But what if it was clean on the outside but dirty on the inside? *(Tip it for them to see into it.)* I don't guess you'd want to drink from it now. Most of us would probably pick the next nicest cup. This one is clean on the inside, but it's dirty on the outside. Still, it's better than the first, isn't it? How about this cup? It isn't as nice as the first two. It's kind of chipped, and it's old. But it's clean on the inside, outside, and all over. This is the cup we would all pick. It doesn't look as nice, but it's the best choice.

A man in the Bible named Simon Peter was having trouble trying to decide who he should tell about Jesus and who he shouldn't. Peter was Jewish and at first thought the good news about Jesus was only for people of his race. But Simon Peter found out that what he thought was wrong. He learned that God accepts all people equally and so should he. When Peter learned this lesson, he exclaimed, "God has shown me that I should not call anyone common or unclean."

This is a lesson all of us need to learn and never forget. God accepts all people equally and so should we. Not accepting a person because they're a different color than you is as silly as drinking out of the first cup, because it's the prettiest on the outside, or not drinking out of the third cup, because it isn't as pretty on the outside. Don't judge people by their race, color, religion, appearance, or any other outside characteristic. God accepts all people equally and so should we.

25
Religious Liberty Sunday

Let Freedom Ring!

Text: Leviticus 25:10, "Proclaim liberty throughout all the land unto all the inhabitants thereof" (KJV).

Main Truth: We should thank God for the privilege of living in a land of freedom and opportunity.

Interest Object: A replica or picture of the Liberty Bell.

This is a picture of the Liberty Bell. The Liberty Bell is a huge iron bell that weighs over a ton and is kept at Independence National Historical Park in Philadelphia, Pennsylvania. I hope all of you go to see it someday. It's over twelve feet around at its base. It was made in 1752 in London. When the founders of our nation signed the Declaration of Independence in 1776 to make America free from England, the Liberty Bell was rung to celebrate our freedom, or liberty which is another word for freedom. When they rang the bell, it cracked, so they had it recast. When they rang it again, it cracked again. This time they just left it cracked. The last time it was rung was on George Washington's birthday in 1846.

The first time I saw the Liberty Bell, I was surprised to see that there was a verse of Scripture on it. This verse is Leviticus 25:10, which says, "Proclaim liberty throughout the land to all the inhabitants thereof" (KJV). To *proclaim* means to tell or announce. Inhabitants are people. So the message from the Bible on the Liberty Bell means to tell everybody who lives in your country about freedom.

That's a good message for us to hear today on Religious Liberty Sunday. This is a day we celebrate being free Americans. The Liberty Bell is a good reminder to each of us that we're free today because other people in the past fought for and won freedom. We should be thankful for those people and what they did. Let's take the verse on the Liberty Bell seriously—tell everybody who lives in your country about freedom.

We should also thank God for the privilege of living in a land of freedom and opportunity. God wants people, all people, to be free. God gives us a lot of different kinds of freedoms. Let's be thankful today for all the freedoms we enjoy, such as being able to worship, think what we please, and say what we think. We should ask God to help us be good citizens of a free land.

26
Revival

How Do We Change?

Text: Psalm 51:10,12, "Create in me a clean heart, O God, and put a new and right spirit within me. Restore to me the joy of thy salvation, and uphold me with a willing spirit."

Main Truth: Revival is a time for change which helps us better our lives.

Interest Object: An old pair of windshield wipers. You can locate these at any garage, service station, or car parts store.

The other day I was driving my car when it started to rain. I turned on my windshield wipers, but, instead of wiping the rain off the windshield, they smeared the water around. It became harder to see rather than easier. I pulled into the first car parts store I came to, took off the old wiper blades which I have here, bought some new blades, and put them on the car. You have to replace windshield wiper blades every now and then. The old blades had become hard and worn out and needed to be changed. The new blades did the job.

We all need a chance to change sometimes. How do we change? This week we're having revival meetings. We have a guest preacher and singer, and we will have a great time together. Revival is a chance for change and an opportunity for renewal. King David prayed in Psalm 51:10,12, "Create in me a clean heart, O God, and put a new and right spirit within me. Restore to me the joy of thy salvation, and uphold me with a willing spirit."

We become tired, and our spirits need to be refreshed. We need to think again and be glad for God and what He does for us. Revival is a time for this. Revival is a time for change which helps us to live better. Come to the revival services this week and see if you don't feel better because you did. I think you will. We all need a change, a new start from time to time. Get yours at revival this week.

27

Senior Adult Day

They've Been Where We Haven't

Text: Leviticus 19:32, "You shall rise up before the hoary head, and honor the face of an old man, and you shall fear your God: I am the Lord."

Main Truth: Let's be thankful for the guidance and wisdom of our senior adults.

I was driving on an interstate highway not long ago. It was a nice, clear day. As I drove along, I noticed some dark clouds in the distance, although it was still sunny and clear where I was. Then I began to notice that cars on the other side of the highway, which were coming toward me, had their lights on. They were wet, too. Some of them had their windshield wipers on. Why? They had been where I was going. I learned from them that up ahead was a storm. I could only guess from looking at the clouds, but by learning from the other cars, I knew what to expect ahead.

As I think about that day on the freeway, I remember many things I've learned from senior adults. They have been where most of us are going in life, so they can help us know what to expect ahead. We need to listen to them and learn from them. They have a lot to teach us.

Today is Senior Adult Day in our church. We owe a lot to our grandparents and the other senior adults of our church. They give us help that comes only with age and experience. Let's be thankful for the guidance and wisdom of our senior members. Let's also take time to say "thank you" and "I love you" to them.

Older people were highly respected in the Bible. This is why Leviticus

19:32 commanded youth to honor the older people. It says, "You shall rise up before the hoary head, and honor the face of an old man, and you shall fear your God: I am the Lord." This means our senior adults deserve our honor, love, and respect. They've been where we haven't!

28
Stewardship Promotion

Put on a Happy Face

Text: 2 Corinthians 9:7, "God loves a cheerful giver."

Main Truth: We should happily give our money to the Lord's work through the church.

Interest Object: A round "smiling face."

Memory Maker: A smiling face sticker for each child. These are available at bookstores and novelty stores.

You know what this is. It's a smiling face. I'm wearing it on my lapel, because today we're talking about and pledging money to our church budget. Maybe some people aren't happy about this. Some folks don't like to talk about money in church or be asked to give or pledge money. They frown about it or put on an unhappy face. I have a different idea about it. I like to talk about money in church, because money is an important part of God's world and work. So, I've put on a happy face by wearing a smiling face sticker to show my happiness that today is Stewardship Sunday.

We should happily give our money to the Lord's work through the church. This isn't just my idea either. Paul, who wrote a lot of the New Testament, wrote quite a bit about money in 2 Corinthians. One of the things he says is, "God loves a cheerful giver." When I think about this verse, 2 Corinthians 9:7, I know God wants me to be happy in what I give and the way I give to the Lord's work. In this verse Paul was telling us that we need to give with the right attitude and that the right attitude is the happy face attitude—cheeriness. Let's smile and be happy that we have money to give to the Lord's work, then let's give as much as we can and be cheerful about it. I believe this is the way God wants us to think about giving money, time, or anything else we have to give.

I have a smiling face sticker for each of you. Let it show that you, too, are putting on a happy face by being a cheerful giver to the work of the Lord through this church. Wear it with pride and happiness.

29
Sunday School Promotion Day

The Girl Who Wouldn't Promote

Text: Ephesians 4:15, "We are to grow up in every way into him who is the head, into Christ."

Main Truth: It's the nature of faith for us to progress.

Once upon a time, there was a girl in the third grade. At Sunday School she loved her third-grade department. She loved the teachers, the Bible stories she learned, and the things they did in the department. She loved everything about her third- grade department. In fact, she loved it so much that when it was time for her to go to the fourth-grade department, she decided she would stay in the third-grade group for another year. So she did. Her parents tried to talk her into promoting to the fourth-grade department Her pastor and even the teachers she loved so much in the third-grade department tried to talk her into promoting. However, she wouldn't budge. So she spent another year in the same department.

When the next year's promotion day came, the same thing happened. And the next year, and the next, and the next. In fact, she stayed in the third-grade department until she was grown . The teachers she loved retired, and the Bible stories were all well known to her by now. All the other children in the third-grade department were third graders who fit in the chairs, heard the Bible stories for the first time, and enjoyed doing things third graders could do. And here was this woman who was in the third-grade department for her fortieth year in a row!

Pretty silly, huh? I mean, who ever heard of a girl who stayed in a third-grade department for forty years? Look at all she would miss, if this really happened. She'd never grow in her knowledge of the Bible, like we're supposed to. She'd miss the fun and fellowship of being with her own age group.

She'd miss the new teachers, ideas, trips, and things in her new department each year. She'd never be able to teach others about God's Word. It would be a shame not to promote to the next class, department, or level each year on this Sunday. It's the nature of faith for us to progress, not to stand still or go backwards, but to go forward. That's why we have different levels in Sunday School. There are different Bible passages to be studied, new ways to learn to live out our faith. We can never stop growing and learning if we want to please God. It's the nature of faith to progress. Like the Bible says in Ephesians 4:15, "We are to grow up in every way into him who is the head, into Christ." So, enjoy your new department, teachers, and stories. This is the way it should be. Then, as you grow you can help others to grow, too. Congratulations on your promotions!

30
Thanksgiving

Everybody but Turkeys Give Thanks

Text: Deuteronomy 8:10, "You shall eat and be full, and you shall bless the Lord your God for the good land he has given you."

Main Truth: If you aren't a turkey, be thankful to God for the blessings of living in this great land.

A pastor was talking to a group of boys and girls on the Sunday before Thanksgiving. He was talking to them about being thankful for good food, homes, families, and all their other blessings. He asked them the following question. "Who should be thankful to God this week?"

A girl raised her hand. The pastor gave her the microphone, and she said, loudly, "Everybody but the turkeys!"

Everybody laughed. But the little girl was exactly right! Everybody, except for the turkeys, should be thankful to God for many blessings. The lesson for us is be thankful for the blessings of living in this great land.

Hundreds of years ago, Moses reminded the Jewish people to be thankful. They were ready to go into the land God had promised them. Moses told the people that God would provide for all their needs. He said, "You shall eat and be full, and you shall bless the Lord your God for the good land he has given you" (Deut. 8:10).

Those words are a reminder to us. This week we will eat until we are full. When we do, let's not forget that it's God who blesses us with food. Let's all give thanks, sincere thanks, true thanks to God for all our blessings.

31
Trinity Sunday

How Do You Picture God?

Text: 2 Corinthians 13:14, "The grace of the Lord Jesus Christ and the love of God and the fellowship of the Holy Spirit be with you all."

Main Truth: We should think of God as one person pictured in three ways in the Bible.

Interest Object: A child's drawing that isn't too recognizable. You can locate one from a Sunday School teacher, parent, or schoolteacher.

How do you picture God? It's hard for us to think about what God is like, because nobody really knows. I brought this drawing by one of my young friends. It reminds me of a story I heard of a little girl in Sunday School who was drawing a picture. Her teacher asked her what she was drawing. "God," she answered.

The teacher said, "No one knows what God looks like!"

The little girl then said, "Well, everyone will when I get through with this picture!"

I like that story. But what the teacher said is true; no one knows what God looks like. What I want you to know about today, when we celebrate Trinity Sunday, is that we should think of God as one person pictured in three ways in the Bible. The Bible presents God as Father, Jesus Christ the Son, and the Holy Spirit. I'm not saying God is three different people or that these are three parts of God. I'm saying that God is one person or being, presented in three ways. This is hard to understand, but this is the way the Bible pictures God.

Somebody once said that God was *for* people in the Old Testament in the person of God the Father, *with* people in the New Testament in the person of Jesus, and *in* people from Pentecost in the person of the Holy Spirit. Genesis 1:1 presents God the Father for the first time in the Bible. Matthew 1 and Luke 2 present Jesus for the first time at his birth. And Acts 2 presents the Holy Spirit for the first time at Pentecost. These are the three ways God is presented in the Bible, and the way we should think of God.

Paul wrote of God in this way. In 2 Corinthians 13:14, Paul closed his letter by writing, "The grace of the Lord Jesus Christ and the love of God and the fellowship of the Holy Spirit be with you all." Paul's prayer for them is my prayer for you. We should think of God as one person pictured three ways in the Bible.

32

Valentine's Day

Horace the Horrible

Text: James 2:8, "If you really fulfil the royal law, according to the scripture, 'You shall love your neighbor as yourself,' you do well."

Main Truth: We must love every person equally, because we're all brothers and sisters.

When I was in the fourth grade, a strange and terrible thing happened in my classroom at school on Valentine's Day. The teacher had put a large cardboard box in the corner of the front of the room for all of us to put valentines in for each other. She had decorated it with red paper and white hearts so it looked pretty. Like my classmates, I went to the store and bought valentines for all the other children. I signed the valentines, put them in envelopes and put a classmate's name on each one. I proudly slipped my valentines for my friends into the decorated box and was excited about the valentines I was going to receive. I was especially hoping for one from a girl for whom I had bought a special valentine, one nicer than all the others.

Oh, I forgot to tell you, there was one boy in my class I didn't like, so I didn't give him a valentine. His name was Horace, and he was different from everybody else in our class. We called him "Horace the Horrible." For one thing, his clothes weren't like ours. They never seemed to fit him right and were always dirty. He smelled bad most of the time, like he didn't bathe or something. He was real small for his age, so everybody picked on him. And sometimes he would fall asleep right in class! Nobody liked Horace.

When Valentine's Day finally arrived, the pretty box was opened. The teacher selected two class members to hand out the valentines. I got one from everybody in the class. I even got the special one I was hoping for from the girl. Horace's valentine wasn't like any of the others. He hadn't even gone to the store and bought valentines. His were all handmade! We all thought that was just like Horace—pretty stupid and cheap.

As the valentines were being handed out, everybody got some except Horace. He didn't get a single one! We all thought that was pretty funny and just what he deserved. We didn't think anything about it when Horace didn't come back to class for about a week.

Boys and girls, every time I think about that Valentine's Day, now that I'm grown, I almost get sick. Now I realize just how unloving and cruel we were to Horace. I found out later that Horace was from one of the poorest families in our town. His clothes didn't fit, because they weren't bought for him. They were hand-me-downs from his older brothers or used clothes somebody gave them. He didn't smell good, because he didn't have running water in his house, so he didn't have a shower like the rest of us did. The reason he was so small and fell asleep so easily was because he often didn't have enough to eat, and hunger robs people of energy and health. The reason Horace made all his valentines for his "friends" was because he didn't have any money to buy them for us. He was so hurt and embarrassed about not getting a single valentine that he stayed away from school for a whole week and didn't want to come back ever.

I'm sorry for what I did to Horace, for what we all did to him. We were the stupid ones for treating him like we did. OK, maybe we were just a bunch of children who didn't know any better. I should have known better, because I was a Christian.

As Christians we're supposed to treat everybody, no matter what they look, act, or smell like, as brothers and sisters. We must love every person equally, because we're all brothers and sisters. Please remember this on Valentine's Day, and every day. The Bible says in James 2:8, "If you really fulfil the royal law, according to the scripture, 'You shall love your neighbor as yourself,' you do well." Do well, by treating everybody you meet with love and kindness!

33

Women's Day

The Strength of Steel

Text: Acts 1:14, "All these with one accord devoted themselves to prayer, together with the women and Mary the mother of Jesus, and with his brothers."

Main Truth: Women are a great strength in the Lord's work through the church.

Interest Object: A small piece of steel reinforcing rod. You can locate a scrap piece from just about any construction site.

This is a piece of steel reinforcing rod. I got it from some workers who are building my new house. Let me tell you how builders use it. They take long pieces of this and tie them together with wire near the ground. Then, after they get them just like they want them, they call for the concrete trucks. The trucks come and pour the concrete on the ground inside what they call forms. These rods are all through the middle of the concrete, making it much stronger than it would be without them. The rods are important to the strength of the new building.

Today is Women's Day in our church. We honor the women who serve the Lord by teaching, praying, serving, leading in many ways, and giving their time, talents, and money to the Lord's work. They're like this steel rod in a way.

Women are a great strength in the Lord's work through the church. They've always been from the time the church began. Women followed Jesus and supported His ministry financially (Luke 8:2-3). They were present at the birthday of the church at Pentecost, when about 120 people were gathered in the upper room waiting to see what would happen next.

The book of Acts names the apostles of Jesus among the 120, and in Acts 1:14 it says, "All these with one accord devoted themselves to prayer, together with the women and Mary the mother of Jesus, and with his brothers."

Women have been and still are strong in the work of the Lord. We're thankful for the women of our church. We especially honor them today.

34

World Hunger Sunday

The House on the Hill

Text: 2 Corinthians 8:13-14, "I do not mean that others should be eased and you burdened, but that as a matter of equality your abundance at the present time should supply their want."

Main Truth: We should give our money and pray for those who don't have enough to eat.

Once there was a family that lived on a high hill in a big house. They were very rich. In fact, the six people in this rich family had one-third of all the money and other wealth in their town of 100 people. The other two-thirds of the money was divided among the other ninety-four people. However, the money wasn't divided so each person had the same amount. Sixty-seven of these ninety-four people were very poor, with fifty-five of them making less than $600 a year. Fifty of them were so poor they didn't even have a house to live in; or if they had a places to live, they were in awful condition with leaky roofs, no indoor bathrooms, no electricity, or no running water. In fact, fifty of them had no clean, safe water to drink. They got all kinds of diseases from their water supply, so they stayed sick a lot and many died young. Forty-seven of them couldn't read or write. Another thirty-five of them would be so hungry they were in danger of starving to death. Most of them would never see a doctor in their entire lives. Most of them would never hear of Jesus.

The rich family in the house on the hill, however, would produce enough food each year to feed themselves and the other ninety-four people. But instead of doing so, they stored their food in big warehouses where much of it spoiled before it could be used. The six people in the house on the hill used up almost half of all the electricity, gas, oil, and other products produced in their town and contributed over half of the waste that had to be done away with. The people in the house on the hill were very fortunate. The other ninety-four people weren't quite so blessed.

Boys and girls, the story of the house on the hill helps us think about what our world would be like if there were only 100 people in it instead of five billion. The rich people in the house on the hill would be people who do have enough money, food, and other things. Many people in America as well as in some other countries have enough. But many people in all countries do not have enough, and in some countries almost everyone does not have enough. They are like the other ninety-four people in the story.

America is a rich and blessed nation. Those of us who have all we need should share our riches with the others all over the world who are needy. This is our focus today—World Hunger Sunday. It's a time to realize that we should give our money and pray for those who don't have enough to eat today. Our special offering will go to hungry people in America and around the world.

My asking you to give to and pray for people who are needy is a truly Christian idea. In 2 Corinthians 8:13-14, Paul asked the wealthy Corinthians to give to the poor at Jerusalem. This is what he said, "I do not mean that others should be eased and you burdened, but that as a matter of equality your abundance at the present time should supply their want." If those who have the ability to give will do it, hunger and suffering will be eased in the world. Let's give so others may live!

35

World Peace Sunday

The Peace Pipe

Text: Psalm 34:14, "Depart from evil, and do good; seek peace, and pursue it."

Main Truth: Let's live in peace with others by doing good, and pray for peace for all.

Interest Object: A peace pipe or picture of one from a magazine or encyclopedia.

This is a Native American peace pipe. I bought it in Pipestone, Minnesota, where they have been made for hundreds of years. It's made from a special clay found in that area. For as long as anybody knows, tribes of Indians would be at war with one another at different times. Then, some of their chiefs would get together and decide not to fight anymore. When this happened, they brought out pipes, such as this one, filled them with tobacco, lit them, then passed them around for all the chiefs to take a puff. This was a sign or symbol of their agreement not to fight anymore. So, they are called peace pipes.

Later, when white settlers and the United States Army fought with the Native American Indians and they agreed to stop fighting with one another, they, too, would smoke a peace pipe.

One of the things our world needs today more than anything else is peace. Wouldn't it be good, if we could lead all the people who are fighting with each other to agree to stop fighting and sit in a huge circle and do something to seal their peace agreement? I know smoking isn't good for you, but if it would bring peace I'd try the peace pipe.

How can we help bring peace to our world? One way is to pray for it.

Another is to live peaceably ourselves with everybody in our homes, schools, and neighborhoods. I know this isn't the complete answer, but at least its a beginning.

The Bible gives us a verse that tells us how to begin living without ugliness between people. It's Psalm 34:14, and it says, "Depart from evil, and do good; seek peace, and pursue it." This is one of those verses where the second part means the same thing as the first part. The second part says, "seek peace." The first part tells us how to seek peace—"Depart from evil, and do good." If we do good and not evil to others, peace is what happens. Let's live in peace with others by doing good, and pray for peace for all.

36

World Prayer Sunday

At the Sound of Your Name

Text: 1 Thessalonians 5:17, "Pray constantly."

Main Truth: God should always be on our minds through prayer.

There's a Bible verse that says, "Pray constantly," (1 Thess. 5:17). What does this verse mean? Does it mean we're to walk around all day with our heads bowed, eyes closed, and hands folded in front of us? Does this mean we're never to do anything else but pray? Are we to stay on our knees all the time in prayer? I don't think so. I think it means God should always be on our minds through prayer.

Let me tell you one way we can practice what this verse says. This week whenever you hear your name called—at home, at school, on the playground, or wherever your are—pray. You won't have to close your eyes, just think a prayer in your mind. Maybe it will be to thank God for something good, ask God to forgive you for a lie you told, or to tell God you need help with something. Whatever you might be thinking about when you hear your name called talk to God about it right then and there, silently.

If we all do this, I think we'll begin to do what the Bible verse for World Prayer Sunday says—"Pray constantly." Let's start right now. Let's pretend I've called each of you by name and you've called my name. *(Bow your head, wait a few seconds, and say "Amen.")*

37
Youth Week

Pretending or Preparing?

Text: Ecclesiastes 11:9, "Rejoice, . . . in your youth, and let your heart cheer you in the days of your youth."

Main Truth: Youth week is a time when our teenagers prepare for church work they'll soon be performing regularly.

This is youth week in our church, a time when our teenagers lead us in Sunday School and worship by taking jobs usually filled by adults of our church. Today in Sunday School you may have had youth teachers either instead of your regular teachers or alongside them. In this service some of our teenagers will be ushers, our youth choir will sing, other teenagers will do what our ministers of music and education usually do, and three of our youths will speak during the time the pastor usually preaches.

Now I want to ask you a question about all this. Do you think our young people are just pretending to be church leaders today, or are they preparing to be church leaders in the near future? I think they're preparing, not pretending.

Anybody can pretend to be somebody they're not. I'll bet some of you pretend. Maybe you put on your mom's or dad's clothes and play dress up, or you play school, or pretend to be someone you've seen on TV. So you know what pretending is. Is this what our youth are doing today, pretending to be pastors, teachers, and deacons?

No. They're doing these jobs in the church today because it won't be much longer before many of them will be doing them as young adults. They need to practice now for what they'll be doing soon. That's why we have youth week—to train young people for service, because they have a lot to offer the church with their gifts and talents. One day you'll be teenagers and doing different jobs during youth week.

Youth week is a time when our teenagers prepare for church work they'll soon be doing regularly. It's a happy, fun week, but it's also a week of hard work and learning. Let's pray for our youth as they lead us this week. Be happy we have such wonderful young people who get this practice. Think about their key verse for youth week. It's Ecclesiastes 11:9, "Rejoice, . . . in your youth, and let your heart cheer you in the days of your youth." It means to be happy you're young.

Index of Scripture Texts

Genesis
  2:15 42
  45:3 33

Leviticus
  19:32 73
  25:10 69

Deuteronomy
  8:10 79

Psalms
  34:14 88
  51:10,12 71
  90:12 61

Proverbs
  16:24 45
  31:28 58

Ecclesiastes
  11:9 .... 38, 91

Jeremiah
  33:14 18

Matthew
  2:11 19
  2:1-12 20

6:33	32
9:36	40
21:1-11	63
26:26-28	50

Mark

4:30-32	35
14:26	51
16:1-7	31

Luke

2:1-14	24
2:1-20	20
2:11	21
15:11-32	26

John

13:1-5,14-15	54

Acts

1:14	84
2:1,4	65
10:28	67

Romans

15:4	22

1 Corinthians

11:23-25	52
11:23-26	49
15:3-4	37

2 Corinthians

8:13-14	86
9:7	75
13:14	80

Index of Scpriture Texts

Galatians
  6:11 44

Ephesians
  4:15 77
  6:18 46

Philippians
  4:4 48
  4:6 47
  4:17 45

Colossians
  3:16 27

1 Thessalonians
  5:17 90

1 Timothy
  3:13 29

James
  2:8 82

1 Peter
  2:1-2 59

Revelation
  14:13 56